# THE
# FINAL CHAPTER-
# LOVE

To Bill
with love and
affection!
Frank, 12/5/13

# THE
# FINAL CHAPTER-
# LOVE

BY

F R A N K   W E S T

ISBN: 1492266639
ISBN-13: 9781492266631
Library of Congress Control Number: 2013916022
CreateSpace Independent Publishing Platform
North Charleston, South Carolina

# ALSO BY FRANK WEST

*From Guilt to the Gift of Miracles*
*Healing Our Anger*
*Healing Our Special Relationships*
*A Case of Mistaken Identity*

I dedicate this little book to my beloved late wife Martha, who taught me the meaning of Love. She was and still remains my collaborator, inspiration, and guide, patiently and gently leading me toward a clearer vision of the Truth.

Frank West
Guilford, Connecticut
Summer 2013

# TABLE OF CONTENTS

# Acknowledgement

I'm grateful for the thoughtful editing of this work by my friend Chad Hardin, musician, composer and master of the written word. Without his efforts—or his sure feel for the tone and cadence of my particular voice—this book could not have come to be.

# Preface

As I approached the end of the ninth decade of this lifetime, I had in no way anticipated that I should do any more writing. I'd considered four small books sufficient.

It turns out I was wrong.

And it was all a result of a weekend visit from my good friend and psychic, Ed Moret.

It happened in this way: As Ed entered my house he cried out, "Oh my God, Frank, your late wife Martha was all over me as I woke up this morning. She was so excited and pleased that I was coming down to visit you! Best of all, she has another message for you. She wants you to write a fifth book and has offered you a title for it: *The Final Chapter—Love.*"

That title sounded just right to me, for recently my thoughts had been focused on the "little gap" that I maintained between myself and my brothers—and between my mind and the Mind of our Creator.

In one of our sessions, Ed saw me standing before a Council of eight robed figures, with a monk in a brown hooded robe holding my "book of life," the pages of which were moving, video-like pictures. It seems the purpose of this scene was to indicate that when I cross over I will have an opportunity to share with the Council a report of what I have done with my life in this lifetime (one of many lifetimes, it seems).

For the last thirty years, I've been following a spiritual path that has enriched my life immensely. And it was my late wife Martha who introduced me to this path and traveled with me upon it until she departed this life eight years ago.

I've enjoyed writing this book because it has helped focus me on my goal in this lifetime—a goal I believe we all share and *all will reach*, when we have learned all the lessons we are called upon to learn.

The following introduction summarizes the thought system I have attempted to practice so devotedly these last thirty years, and which can lead us *all* to that goal; i.e., the final chapter, which is Love.

# Introduction

For readers who have not become students of the spiritual path I mentioned—*A Course in Miracles*—a brief outline of its metaphysical basis might be helpful. 'Miracle,' by the way, is defined as "when an ancient hatred has become a present love."(T-26.IX.6:1)[1]

Over forty years ago, Helen Schucman, psychologist and professor at Columbia University's College of Physicians and Surgery, a self-described atheist, began hearing a "voice." The first thing it said to her was, "Write this down… 'This is a course in miracles.'" Terrified, she consulted her boss, Bill Thetford, who encouraged her to do as the voice asked her, and to bring the results to him for evaluation. And if the material sounded psychotic (as Helen feared), he would find a way for her to be helped.

---

1 *A Course in Miracles* consists of a Text, a Workbook for Students, a Manual for Teachers, and two supplemental pamphlets—*Psychotherapy: Purpose, Process and Practice* and *The Song of Prayer*. Taking (T-26.IX.6:1) as an example of an annotation referencing the Course, *T* stands for Text, *26* is the chapter number, the roman numeral *IX* is the section within the chapter, *6* is the paragraph number of that section, and *1* is the sentence number within the paragraph.

It took many months for Helen to begin scribing what came to be known as "the Course." (And some years later, after the Course had been completed, two more works were also scribed: *Psychotherapy: Purpose, Practice and Process;* and *The Song of Prayer,* which dealt with prayer, forgiveness and healing.)

The Course is a highly sophisticated, psychologically astute, and uncompromisingly non-dualistic document whose purpose is to help us identify and undo ideas we have learned from the world that have brought us only pain and misery. It describes the world's existential thought system of sin, guilt and fear (the Ego); and the peace-creating thought system of compassion and Divine Love, symbolized in the world by forgiveness. A third part of all our minds is the capacity to choose between these two systems of thought. The undoing of self-condemnation (guilt), of the resulting illusion of separation from and hatred of our brothers, and of the insane horror of our fear of love, is a step-by-step process.

A crucial tool in this work of undoing is the awareness of the function of *projection*. By means of this psychological process, we seek to regain our innocence by dumping our guilt upon someone or something outside us. This is a futile process that always fails. Projection is the source of our view of the world. As it says in the Course, "The world you see is what you gave it… the outward picture of an inward condition." (T-21.IV.1:2,5)

A fundamental idea in the Course is that only love is real (reality being defined as that which never changes), and all else—whatever in the world we see, including all our bodies—is illusory.

Instead of trusting the holy healing power of eternal love in our own minds—thereby choosing to feel incomplete, lonely and deprived—we seek to manipulate and exploit other figures in the world in order to gather the love we think we need. We hope that by doing so we can alleviate that painful sense of loneliness and incompleteness—that sense of inadequacy that every one of us experiences.

This mistaken process only serves to *increase* our guilt. That is because we know it is not loving. It always leads to guilt, disappointment and rage, much of which is repressed and thus blocked from our awareness. The result is great harm—to our bodies, our minds and all our human relationships.

# 1
# The Wrong Mind

This *seeming* part of our mind contains ideas we have made up. These ideas are not real, but they certainly seem so to us. They seem to come with us at birth. The ancient Chinese recognized this when they created a myth to explain the reason for the founder of Taoism Lao-tzu's serenity and loving peacefulness. According to this myth, Lao-tzu was spared the anguish of infancy and childhood by emerging from his mother's womb as an old man, beard and all! Thus he escaped the damage to the mind that results from the helpless dependency of childhood.

In our own time, the psychoanalyst of the British Object Relations school, Melanie Klein, based her treatment of children on the same premise. She imagined what a new-born infant (who had already responded to external stimuli while *in utero*) might experience when deprived of food or nurture. The helpless child experiences a terror of starvation or abandonment, generating rage at the mother or other care provider. Yet consider its dilemma when it experiences the inevitable fear, rage and hatred at the provider who fails to give the nutrients it requires for physical survival. It's not a  small matter to the infant (or small child). It's a matter of life or death.

But what is the child to do with the resulting hatred? Certainly it must be repressed; for if the child expressed it, he would face the life-threatening danger of rejection, abandonment and consequent death. The one sure result of all this is guilt, for unless hatred is directed outward, the only choice left is to direct it toward one's self. Another word for self-hate is guilt, and that idea is established at the outset of our lives as helpless infants, dependent upon others in the world to supply our needs. We can thus correctly say, guilt comes with birth. *A Course in Miracles* posits a mythological explanation for this primal guilt. The myth is that we took seriously a "tiny, mad idea" that we could possibly separate ourselves from the divine love of Oneness that is our Source.

I once observed a video made by the Yale psychologist Paul Blum, and his wife. Three infants, under the age of twelve months, were sitting in a row. One of the babies reached out and pinched the cheek of the baby next to it, who howled in pain. The baby who had pinched then looked fearfully about, seemingly afraid someone might have observed its cruelty. So self-blame seems to come with the "original equipment."

Since it seems that our first identification of who we are is based on the idea "I am a body separate from other bodies"—bodies on whom we are totally dependent—our happiness and, indeed, our very lives seem to depend upon whether we are recognized, cherished and tenderly cared for. What we might call our *psychological* body is thus at risk, as well as our physical body.

In the 1950s, when I first began the study of psychology, there was told an apparently true story of an orphanage hospital in Latin America that did an experiment. It seems this hospital had an abundance of newborn babies. The experiment involved one group of babies provided with warm, affectionate nurses who, when they fed and changed their babies, talked to them lovingly and played with them briefly. The second group was not treated in this way: the nurses merely changed their diapers and, with a minimum of care, mechanically and dispassionately fed them. The nutrients and physical care given for both groups were identical.

After several months, the results were startling. The first group of babies thrived. They laughed, smiled and made eye contact. The babies in the second group swiftly became listless, dull-eyed, and seemed to be lacking in any will to live, to the point where all finally gave up the wish to feed and died.

A cruel experiment, you might say, but a highly significant one. We could infer that without the expression of loving care, the babies in the second group gave themselves up to despair, and, by refusing to feed, chose suicide. They gave up. (By the way, I can find no record of this event. However, it mimics the studies of rhesus monkeys deprived of their mothers done by Harry F. Harlow in the 1950s.)[2]

Most murders are of inter-family origin. A husband enraged at a wife who leaves him, or "betrays" him, and, in his mind, humiliates him by withholding love from him—rejecting him. In our culture, this leads to much wife-battering. Some cultures actually approve of a father who evicts from his home a

2 "Love in Infant Monkeys," 1959.

daughter as young as eight or ten who has been the victim of rape. The father, mother and child are shamed. Sometimes in their shame the parents order their own child's murder, often by a brother.[3]

Shame is self-hate. The same shame and humiliation motivates a father in some cultures to order a daughter murdered whose crime is deciding whom she wishes to marry instead of marrying the man her family has chosen. The same guilt is evidenced in more "developed" cultures when parents blame themselves unfairly for behavior they disapprove of in their children. They make the mistake of attacking their children because they reflect badly on themselves.

This wrong mind was succinctly expressed by the 14th century Sufi poet Hafiz in the following poem:

> Once a young woman said to me, "Hafiz, what is the sign of someone who knows God?"
> I became very quiet, and looked deep into her eyes, then replied,
> "My dear, they have dropped the knife. Someone who knows God has dropped the cruel knife that most so often use upon their tender self and others."[4]

Hafiz is describing vicious guilt; it is indeed a very cruel knife. Jesus in his Course labels guilt one of the "unholy Trinity"[5] of sin, guilt and fear. Sin can be defined as a sense of either inadequacy or being "bad," as a consequence of a belief in separation.

---

3  Nicholas Kristof: *Half the Sky*, 2012.
4  Daniel Ladinsky: *A Year with Hafiz*
5  Ken Wapnick's term.

Either way, it is cruel self-judgment made by the "wrong mind." There's a sense of "something is missing," "something is not right with me," "I'm not worthy." Personality thus becomes an attempt to develop defenses in order to neutralize these inner states which are totally unconscious. Schemes of behavior are used to attempt to bring peace to such states of mind.

# 2
# The Right Mind

The metaphysics of the Course posits that there is only one reality and that is Love; i.e., Divine Love. It declares unequivocally that, "The recognition of God is the recognition of yourself. There is no separation of God and His creation" (T-8.V.2:7,8); and "God's oneness and ours are not separate because His Oneness encompasses ours." (T-8.V.3:1).

Thus, what we have called the wrong mind is really no mind; it is an illusion we have made and believed is real, even though we seem to have brought its ideas with us at birth, originating in our mistaken identification with our body.

So, if the only reality is Eternal Love, of which we are a part, all else is a dream we made up. "My mind is part of God's. I am very holy"(W-35) describes compassion as our true essence. If this be so, we come into the world bringing with us that holy essence of compassion. Is there any evidence of this?

It seems there might be. The aforementioned psychologist Paul Blum has made some studies that seem to indicate at least empathy and perhaps compassion on the part of infants and toddlers. I have witnessed two videos that I believe show an early capacity for compassion through a simple act of kindness.

The first video opened with a mother and what seemed to be a two year old child standing in the shadows of a corner of a room. A man entered carrying a huge load of books. He walked over to a closet door and attempted to open it. He found he was unable to do so, fumbling futilely with the knob. After perhaps half a minute, the child silently left its mother, walked across the room, and without a word turned the knob and opened the door of the closet for the man standing helplessly before it. The child then turned and silently returned to its mother.

The second video I witnessed began in the same manner with the mother and child in a remote corner of the room. In this instance, a man walked in, again burdened with a load of some kind. He dropped his keys on the floor and stood considering how he might retrieve them while so encumbered. Again, after only a brief moment or two, the small child walked over, picked up the keys and handed them to the man, then turned and silently joined its mother.

Now I trust that no adult had directed these children to act as they did (I trust that the Yale psychology department was not so blatantly fraudulent as to do so), and that the mother was blindfolded and thus unable to send visual signs to her child. If my trust is justified, it seems as if we have evidence that the Course's view of our inborn essence of compassion is correct. All the major religions promote in some form a moral idea such as is set forth in the "Golden Rule" of the New Testament—"Do unto others as you would have them do unto you."

In a recent issue of the *New York Times* (May 5, 2010), another two experiments of Paul Blum were featured.

In the first experiment a one year old child watched two puppets. One puppet behaved in a kindly manner; the other puppet behaved selfishly. Treats were then placed before each puppet, and both treats and puppets placed near enough for the child to reach them. When this happened, the child immediately took the treat from the "bad" puppet, and struck him violently.

In a second experiment, babies under ten months old witnessed one colored block moving up an inclined ramp. At times a second block of a different color helped push the first block up the slope. At other times a separately colored block tried to block the "climbing" block from proceeding up the incline. When the children were then offered both blocks to play with, they overwhelmingly chose the "good guy" block. In this experiment the parents holding the children, and the experimenters, were both blind to the moment of the children choosing the "good guy" block. Similarly, one toddler smacked the "bad guy" block. The colors of the blocks were also found to be irrelevant to the choice the babies made.

Finally, the experimenters found that many babies under one year of age, when near a baby in distress, will reach out to touch or stroke the sufferer, or hand them a bottle. The article states, "Glimmers of moral thought, moral judgment and moral feeling seem to appear even in the first year of life."

In addition, an added blessing concerning the right mind is the fact that not only do we arrive here with a part of the Mind of God, but there is an active energy helping us that the Course calls the Great Rays. "The cornerstone of God's creation is you, for His thought system is light. Remember the Rays that are unseen. The more you approach the center of His thought system, the clearer the light becomes." (T-11.Intro.3:2-4) "Not one light in Heaven but goes with you. Not one Ray that shines forever in the Mind of God but shines on you. Heaven is joined with you in your advance to Heaven...You have found your brother, and you will light each other's way. And from this light will the Great Rays extend back into darkness and forward into God, to shine away the past and so make room for His eternal Presence, in which everything is radiant with light." (T-18.8:1-3,6,7)

We have not been left alone to deal with the darkness in the world, nor in our self-made inner darkness that we think is real. The Great Rays are symbols of the Holy Spirit's power, the voice that speaks for God, the memory we have of that perfect Oneness of Heaven. Being aware of this truth, I wrote on the cover of my first book, "If you knew Who walks beside you on the way that you have chosen, fear would be impossible." (T-18.III.3:2)

# 3
# Healing the Unhealed Mind

I can only teach what I myself have experienced, and I do so by sharing the story of my own journey.

Sixty-five years ago I sought relief from my misery by choosing to enter a twenty-year process of psychoanlysis. That experience taught me that the source of my unhappiness was in ideas about myself and others that I had decided to believe. During that process, I learned to look within, and to have the courage to admit that I had some very dark thoughts about myself; further, I was projecting those dark thoughts upon others; in essence, self-righteously judging and attacking them via projection.

Upon reflection, I see now that as valuable as my twenty years of psychoanalysis was, something essential was missing from the process. What was missing was the "spiritual" dimension of my mind. As Jesus reportedly said to Helen Schucman, "Freud knew a bad thing when he saw it. What he didn't know was, it wasn't real!"

The liberating thing about the Course is its uncompromising insistence that only love is real, and that all other ideas are illusions that we have made up, as a result of our insane fear of love. Its message is that our essence, our reality, is that eternal love. And by undoing our ego thoughts, we allow it to shine outwards from our minds, in all its innocence. It extends this love to all our brothers and sisters.

Our "special function" of extending love to others brings us our only happiness: "Such is the Holy Spirit's kind perception of specialness; His use of what you made, to heal instead of harm. To each He gives a special function in salvation he alone can fill; a part for only him. Nor is the plan complete until he finds his special function, and fulfills the part assigned to him, to make himself complete within a world where incompletion rules." (T-25.VI.4)

So what are the essential steps to attaining this happiness, this inner peaceful stillness?

Again, I can only share my experience. I suggest, dear reader, that you experiment with what I offer here; and if it works, use it. If not, seek your own form of practice. There is but one content (mind) with the same goal (peace); and many forms (behavior) to reach that goal.

Since each of us is different in form, our process may vary in form. But be assured our minds are all the same. This sameness of content is the basis for our joining both with our Source, and with all our brothers.

I consider the following steps to be crucial for the purpose of healing my mind:

1) A constant vigilance as to what my mood is at any moment.
2) A wish to have freedom from the pain of guilt, anger, fear, hate and depression.

3) A deep yearning for the stillness and peace of a *forgiven* mind; and for the quiet joy of a *forgiving* mind.

4) An awareness and understanding of the apparent three-part mind (Egotism, Love and the Decision Maker), with the blessing of the power to choose love for ourselves.

5) A deep willingness to swiftly say "No" to attack thoughts, thoughts of victimhood, thoughts of self-blame, shame or guilt. That is to say, a willingness to bring our dark thoughts to the Light of Truth in our minds, and to ask the Holy Spirit or Jesus (or whatever figure symbolizes Love for us) to look at them with us—so that Love's merciful vision can shine the dark thoughts away. The result is a forgiving mind.

6) A patience with the process, including an awareness that once we decide to listen to the right mind, there is a temptation to flee from love back to wrong-minded thoughts. As Jesus puts it in his Course, "When the light (love) draws nearer, you rush to darkness, sometimes to lesser forms of fear, and sometimes to stark terror" (T-18.III.2:1); or, "Your fear of attack is nothing compared to your fear of love" (T-13.III.2:3); and also, "You associate love with weakness and hatred with strength, and your own real power seems to you as your real weakness. For you could not control your joyous response to the call of love if you heard it, and the whole world you thought you made would vanish. The Holy Spirit, then, seems to be attacking your fortress, for you would shut out God, and He does not will to be excluded." (T-13.III.3.2-4)

7) A fundamental state of mind needed during this healing process is trust: Trust in the overwhelming eternal power of love, trust that all those vicious dark thoughts we make cannot extinguish the eternal light; trust that the outcome (our happiness) is "as certain as God" (T-12.III.3:10).

8) A regular period of prayer or meditation at the start and ending of each day is an important means for doing the work of changing the mind. One form is given at the end of Lesson 137 in the Workbook:

"Yet must we be prepared for such a gift. And so we will begin the day with this, and give ten minutes to these thoughts with which we will conclude today at night as well:

*When I am healed I am not healed alone. And I would share my healing with the world, that sickness may be banished from the mind of God's one Son, Who is my only Self.*

Let healing be through you this very day. And as you rest in quiet, be prepared to give as you receive, to hold but what you give, and to receive the Word of God to take the place of all the foolish thoughts that ever were imagined. Now we come together to make well all that was sick, and offer blessing where there was attack. Nor will we let this function be forgot as every hour of the day slips by, remembering our purpose with this thought:

*When I am healed I am not healed alone. And I would bless my brothers, for I would be healed with them, as they are healed with me.*" (W-137.14,15)

9) It may also be helpful to form a group of other students of the Course, for the motivation to change is strengthened through the shared interests of others who are dealing with the same issues as you are. There is also great value in the inspiration we receive as we hear evidence of the healing of a group member's mind. It helps us develop trust in the process in which we are engaged. And if you should choose to gather a group of persons with the purpose of joint study of the Course, you will be blessed by the truth that you learn what you teach. That certainly has been my experience, which is why I continue to teach the Course. "Giving and receiving are the same." (W-108).

10) A final and truly fundamental means to advance healing is a determination to give over the direction of your life to the "voice for God," as clearly described in the last five lessons of the Workbook:

**"This holy instant would I give to You.**
**Be You in charge. For I would follow You,**
**Certain that Your direction gives me peace.**
And if I need a word to help me, He will give it to me. If I need a thought, that will He also give. And if I need but stillness and a tranquil, open mind, these are the gifts I will receive of Him. He is in charge by my request. And He will hear and answer me, because He speaks for God my Father and His holy Son." (W-361 thru 365)

As an example of this decision to trust the Holy Spirit's direction of one's life, I've asked one student of the Course to describe an incident from his life which can serve as an inspiration to us all:

## Trusting God, Trusting My Brother

I am a professional musician. I am also a student of *A Course in Miracles*. I began studying the Course in 1989, yet I don't feel my authentic understanding and practice of the Course began until I began working with Frank West in 1998.

Over the last several months, I have made a very particular and determined practice out of the idea of "giving my life to God." As I have done so, my life more and more seems to unfold by itself—and with a sense of order and beauty and rightness that I could never have conceived of out of my own, so-called, understanding.

Some months ago I was music-directing a local production of the musical *Annie*. I had assembled an orchestra pit of 11 professional musicians to play for this production. Two weeks before our opening performance, the drummer I had engaged had to withdraw. I scrambled to find a replacement, yet none of the professional drummers in the area were available.

One of these professional drummers, named Rick, suggested that I hire a student of his to play the show. It was a high school student. Rick said he felt the kid was up to doing it.

A few hours later the kid called me. His name was Derek. He was only sixteen years old, and had never played a musical before in his life. Yet he seemed determined to do it. I heard myself agreeing, against my better judgment, to bring the drum score by his house so that he could study it.

You have to understand how important the drummer is in a show like *Annie*. He is the 'rhythmic motor' for the entire orchestra, and a drummer can make or break a performance. The hard-and-fast rule of musical theatre pits: *Never hire anyone as your drummer who isn't an experienced professional!* A weak drummer will literally destroy your pit.

The next morning I began writing in my journal. I have kept a journal regularly over the last 20 years; and in this journal a voice—which I would describe as "the still, small voice," yet which I personally experience as the person known as Jesus—speaks to me. Sometimes I ask it a question, and it answers. Or it merely begins to speak, and I write as if I were taking dictation.

The morning after Derek had called me, the voice said this:

*Be not afraid. Neither be you anxious. Derek is sent to you. Receive him as the holy Son of God he is. Let the perfection of your pit unfold.*

*All of your life you have been afraid of trusting your brothers, of trusting yourself, and of trusting me. Therefore you hid from life.*

*Let go now. You have relinquished all control. Merely "show up." I will do the rest.*

The next day Jesus offered further reassurance:

*Give the pit and the rehearsals and the performances to me. Give the manifesting of the drummer to me as well. As I told you, Derek is sent to you—Yet it is not yours to divine what the gifts are you are to exchange. Have trust in this unfolding. You will have a fine drummer for the performance.*

The next day I met with Derek to play through the score for the first time. I met with a boy who had turned sixteen just two weeks before, yet who looked younger than that. A sophomore in high school who had never before played a musical! Yet at the same time, there was in him this openness, and a determination that seemed fearless to me.

We spent two and a half hours going through the first act. His playing during this rehearsal did not blow me away. It was pretty much there, but with none of the finesse or clear contours that a good performance would demand. Yet I noticed two remarkable things at the end of that rehearsal: first, he had been intensely present during every second of that two hours—his mind had followed every turn in the score, had apprehended every direction I had given, every comment I had made. It had not faltered or wandered for one second. He had been "with me" the whole time. This was a level of attention rare even in a professional musician. The second thing I noticed: Even though we'd worked nonstop for two and a half hours, I felt energized, inspired, uplifted by the experience. I had more energy at the end of the rehearsal than at the start.

The next morning I wrote in my journal:

"Master, thank you for my time with Derek. I place this in your hands. I ask for your guidance."

*Derek is your teacher, Chad. A model of openness and innocence. He is you. You are also that openness and innocence. Trust what you are—and bring it to all your endeavors—all your relationships.*

*Follow my guidance. You yet have a gift for Derek.*

*Listen today for my guidance. Expect only miracles.*

Later that day I rehearsed the second act with Derek. He showed the same openness, quiet courage and unwavering attention. Yet by the end of the rehearsal, I still had no clue how Derek would do in an actual performance of a complex musical, with ten other musicians—whether he would actually be able to cut it. I called his father in so that he could hear what I had to say to Derek. I told him he was taking on a huge job; and if, after going to bed that night, he woke up in the middle of it in a cold sweat asking himself, "What have I done, thinking that I could learn a show at the last minute and then go in and play it?"—well, I said that it would be more than all right with me if he withdrew, that I would have no problem finding a replacement; and that I would have nothing other than total respect for his decision, and gratitude that I'd had the privilege of meeting such a remarkable guy.

You see, the human part of my mind *wanted* him to withdraw, because it was terrified that he would come in and ruin my pit, and make a fool out of me! Yet I could see by his cool reaction to what I said that he wouldn't even consider withdrawing—he was in it for the long haul.

The next morning I wrote in my journal:

"Thank you, Master—For my open heart of yesterday. And for sending me Derek. I love him!"

*And he responds to your love. You have joined on a level much deeper than a sexual joining. Cherish that. Seek that level with him, without turning away—without fleeing from Love's boundless brightness. Seek this level—or rather, do not* seek, *but open your heart to the awareness of the eternal jointure with your brothers—with all of your pit—and with your singers; and with everyone you meet or think of.*

*Give your relationships to God. Let them be, therefore, what they are; and not what you would make of them. You would make of these relationships something less than Everything.*

19

A few days later, Jesus added this:

*Let the Life be. You are returning it to God. You are returning yourself to God, which is where you have always been in truth.*

*Give Him every decision. Give Him each performance of every pit member. Your only function is to be there, present to the Life—letting it flow, open to it, knowing that you are It.*

*Such is Derek's teaching to you. That openness, that direct joining, without an interposing ego (which is judgment, which is separation). You had thought that joining with the allness of Life would overwhelm and destroy you. You now see it exhilarates. This is the life more abundant.*

*There is nothing to fear!*

*Give this day to God, and be happy.*

A week later, Derek came in for a rehearsal with partial pit, and—the next night—the full pit. The first performance was the following night. He played beautifully. He seemed to know instinctively how to lead and follow simultaneously, which is the mark of a seasoned musician. And with each performance, his playing became more controlled, more refined. A miracle really. I've already hired him to play my next show.

As end to the story, here is what Jesus said the morning after our final performance:

*Listen today. Address each task remembering that you have given it to God: and that you are simply listening, and witnessing its unfolding. You need do nothing. Your sole responsibility is to keep giving the task to God (each time you forget), under my control. I intercede within the dream of the world, between the false will you made, and the Will of our Father; which is the true will, and also your will. Thus the shadows of this illusory world you made begin to reflect the One Will—and therefore is His Will done on earth, as it is in heaven.*

*All else too: listen in confidence to the Father, and with me in absolute control. So with your friendship with Derek, a kindred soul. With him, you have a holy relationship, based on joining, and true friendship. Do not turn away from him—he will not turn away from you. He is teaching you how to stand in the presence of love with a simple and open heart—without guilt or fear.*

*Be grateful for him.*

* * *

11. A final help in motivating myself toward the goal of a healed mind is the truth that it is the will of God that we make the right choice, the choice for Love:

> "Hear me, my brothers, hear and join with me. God has ordained I cannot call in vain, and in His certainty I rest content. For you *will* hear, and you *will* choose again. And in this choice is everyone made free.
>
> I thank You, Father, for these holy ones who are my brothers as they are Your Sons. My faith in them is Yours. I am as sure that they will come to me as You are sure of what they are, and will forever be. They will accept the gift I offer them, because You gave it me on their behalf. And as I would do Your holy Will, so will they choose. And I give thanks for them." (T-31.VIII.9:4-7,10:1-6)

# 4
# The Final Chapter

When one has successfully undone the self-destructive, separating ideas of the wrong mind, one experiences what the Course calls the "Happy Dream" (T-18.V), followed by a state of mind called the "Real World." (W-p II.8) The process has led one to the top of the spiritual ladder. Through accepting forgiveness (actually an awareness that there has been *nothing to forgive*), one has progressed upward toward what the Course calls "the lawns outside Heaven's gate." (T-31.VIII.9:3; C-3.4:9) The idea of separation from our brothers and our separation from God have weakened to become almost non-existent. "What remains is peace eternal and the Will of God." (C-6:9)

The world, which had been seen as a classroom for learning the liberation of Truth, is now seen as a shining reflection of the love of God:

> "Beyond the body, beyond the sun and stars, past everything you see and yet somehow familiar, is an arc of golden light that stretches as you look into a great and shining circle. And all the circle fills with light before your

eyes. The edges of the circle disappear, and what is in it is no longer contained at all. The light expands and covers everything, extending to infinity forever shining and with no break or limit anywhere. Within it everything is joined in perfect continuity. Nor is it possible to imagine that anything could be outside, for there is nowhere that this light is not.

This is the vision of the Son of God, whom you know well. Here is the sight of him who knows his Father. Here is the memory of what you are; a part of this, with all of it within, and joined to all as surely as all is joined in you. Accept the vision that can show you this, and not the body. You know the ancient song, and know it well. Nothing will ever be as dear to you as is this ancient hymn of love the Son of God sings to his Father still.

And now the blind can see, for that same song they sing in honor of their Creator gives praise to them as well. The blindness that they made will not withstand the memory of this song. And they will look upon the vision of the Son of God, remembering who he is they sing of. What is a miracle but this remembering? And who is there in whom this memory lies not? The light in one awakens it in all. And when you see it in your brother, you *are* remembering for everyone." (T-21.I.8,9,10)

The closest I have come to experiencing something like this poetic expression of "oneness" was during a recent interaction with a patient of mine. She was projecting her self-hate upon me in what I can only describe as a full-blown fury of hatred.

As I chose to see beyond her rage—perceiving instead only a cry for love, a desperate, anguished cry of pain—I felt a sense of a quiet joining with her. I experienced a peaceful compassion. I felt I had joined with her on another level entirely. And the astounding thing about those moments was that in the very midst of her furious rage (as this woman told me later), she perceived my face as shining with a radiance of which I had absolutely no awareness. At one point, she was unable to distinguish my facial features, the radiance was so bright. My interpretation of this is that this woman experienced the Christ presence even in the midst of her hate. And *my* contribution to this event was merely to stay in my right mind and thus allow the Holy Spirit's healing to occur. I chose defenselessness (W-135, 153), and in that moment the illusion of separation was dispelled.

When we choose Love's vision rather than our egos, we are enabled to see the Face of Christ not only in ourselves, but in *all* our brothers. (T-26.IX) We have awakened to the awareness that all of us have all along the return "journey" been forgiven for what we have *not done*. We see that nothing has happened and have become "willing to forgive the Son of God for what he did not do." (T-17.III.1:5)

I can in no way presume that I have arrived at the Final Chapter. That would be a denial of the truth. Yet I sense I am approaching it—certainly, I'm much closer than that day eighty-seven years ago when I chose to enter this illusory lifetime, along with a guilty sense of "something is lacking in me." I marvel now at the memory of hearing the words, "You are just visiting for a while and don't belong here" that I heard at age six as I played with my toy trucks and cars beneath the back porch.[6] That moment I, of course, forgot—only to be reminded of it when I first read the words…

> "This world you seem to live in is not home to you. And somewhere in your mind you know this is true. A memory of home keeps haunting you, as if there were a place that called you to return…"
> (W-182.1:1-3)

No, I've not yet allowed myself the vision of the Real World. Yet I was startled a few years ago while on a ten-day cruise with friends, sailing in the Aegean. The weather was perfect, the wind and water couldn't have been more lovely, the evening sunset—dinners on one Greek island after another with good friends—all could not be more pleasant. Yet what startled me was that right from the moment we got on the boat until the jet back home took off from Athens airport, I kept hearing my recollection of words from the Course: "Leave the world—you never wanted it!" The actual quote is…

> "Give up the world! But not to sacrifice. You never wanted it."
> (T-30.9:3-6)

My experience there in the turquoise-colored Aegean was thankfully free of any sense of sacrifice or loss. I'd given up any need for the world to be what I thought it needed to be to meet my perceived needs. That idea is a crucial teaching of the Course. When I think about it, it reflects the words I heard at age 6 as I

---

6  I write at some length about this incident from my childhood in my book *From Guilt to the Gift of Miracles*.

26

played under the porch, telling me that this world is not my true home. Only the above quote from the Course goes much deeper: At the top of the spiritual ladder, there is an awareness that all specifics—*all* the specifics of the universe (or universes)—vanish into nothingness. Only Love remains as we merge with that Oneness…

Before, it was difficult for us to conceive of the truth that the world is an illusion, a projection from the one Wrong Mind. Now in quiet joyfulness we are entitled to see beyond all appearances (T-31.9:1) to see the shining glory of a forgiven world. (T-17.II)

We are not yet home, but we are on the cusp of being drawn into that "Oneness joined as One" (T-25.I.6), that indescribable presence of Divine Love. We become aware that indeed we actually had never left that home. We only dreamed we had.

There is an image that I find helpful in considering these matters, and it comes from the opening of one of the supplement *The Song of Prayer*:

> "Prayer is the greatest gift with which God blessed His Son at his creation. It was then what it is to become; the single voice Creator and creation share; the song the Son sings to the Father, Who returns the thanks it offers Him unto the Son. Endless the harmony, and endless, too, the joyous concord of the Love They give forever to Each Other. And in this, is creation extended. God gives thanks to His extension in His Son. His Son gives thanks for his creation, in the song of his creating in his Father's name. The Love they share is what all prayer will be throughout eternity, when time is done."
> (S-I.1:1-7)

I envision the Great Rays shining in golden light upon all sons of God—those passed by, those now present in the world, and all those yet unborn. These Rays symbolize the joyful song of gratitude of the Creator for all the created sons of God. And the Great Rays shine from the sons of God to our Source, and to each other.

The song of gratitude we sing in reply to our Creator can be symbolized in an adaptation I use of the prayer found in the Workbook's Lesson 232:

> Hear my prayer of gratitude, Father, that I and all my brothers are a part of Your Divine Mind.
>
> Hear my song of joy that your Great Rays of gratitude shine endlessly upon myself and all my brothers.
>
> We rejoice that we all, at any moment, may choose to dwell with You.
>
> Our hearts overflow with happiness that we never left You and You never left us. What joy that our voices join in the sweet harmony with Yours, creating that blessed union of peace!

Such a prayer illustrates the quote, "What shares a common purpose is the same." (T-27.VI.1:5) The common purpose is gratitude found. The result is love. The Father rejoices that the Son yearns to return to Him, and the Son rejoices that his loving Father yearns for his return. Their song has one note—gratitude, the highest form of prayer, True Prayer. (S-I) There is no entreaty here because there is no need—all is abundance!

After we forgot to laugh at the tiny, mad idea that we could ever separate from our Creator's love, we made a "little gap" (T-28.III.7:1) between our Creator and a portion of His Mind we retained. And into that gap we placed ideas of separation, guilt, sin and fear. The process of undoing these ideas through forgiveness has resulted in a vacuum into which love rushed in to fill the gap. A joyful state of a "stillness and a tranquil open mind" resulted. (W-361.1:3) Fortunately we had retained a memory of a home that called to us to return (W-82.1:1-3), and now we have done so because we chose "a forgiving mind." (W-97)

The resulting Real World (W-8) has a number of characteristics. In essence, it can be described as a state of mind that envisions a forgiven world. (T-17.II) "Nothing that you remember that made your heart sing with joy has ever brought you even a little part of the happiness this sight will bring you" (T-17.II.1:5) This happiness results from your seeing the Son of God—the Face of Christ—in all your brothers, for you will be able to see beyond all forms and appearances. As Jesus puts it in Chapter 30:

> "And you will see the Christ in him because you let Him come to you. And when He has appeared to you, you will be certain you are like Him, for He is the changeless in your brother and in you. This you will look upon when you decide there is not an appearance you would hold in place of what your brother really is." (T-30.VIII.5:8-9,6:1)

I have another example from my life that points in the direction of this last Course quote.

There came to me in my practice as a marriage and family therapist a couple who were in trouble. The husband was a very frightened and therefore very angry man with a decidedly unforgiving mind, "afraid and angry, weak and blustering…does not ask, because it thinks it knows. It does not question, certain it is right."

(W-121.3:1,5:4,5)

His wife was terrified of his rages and need to control her. At the outset, it was clear to me that the husband was a man whose hatred was murderous (an intuition that I later learned was true, for he had threatened to murder his previous therapist, and the therapist's wife and children. The therapist had resorted to a legal restraining order for his family's protection).

When I was with this patient, my unhealed mind experienced fear of my own murder, especially on occasions when I heard his maniacal laughter as he left my office. As a consequence, my frightened heart prevented me from having any real compassion for him.

It thus became apparent to me that there was no healing occurring as a result of my mistaken choice of fear. Consequently, this patient was in control of the "therapy" sessions—which, of course, was his intent, as it had been with his previous therapist also.

Finally I decided the only solution was for me to return to my right mind. So prior to his next 8 a.m. appointment, I decided to awaken at 3 a.m. and spend the next five hours in prayer and meditation, asking the Holy Spirit to disappear my terror with His healing love. I was *determined* to give up my fear of death. I saw in that process that the problem had been my mistaken identification with my body as my self. I grew increasingly determined to accept instead my true identity as Spirit. I meditated on the quote:

> "Spirit am I, a holy Son of God, free of all limits, safe and healed and whole, free to forgive, and free to save the world." (W-97.7:2)

As a consequence of my efforts to undo the terror I had been choosing, I now felt a defenseless serenity that—should my patient indeed murder my body—I would still remain "healed and whole." I had chosen to shift my identity to the right mind and ally myself with Eternal Love.

As I walked into that session I was a different person. I said nothing. I did nothing. But I saw my patient differently because I saw myself differently. I now perceived his terror, and resulting need to control through hatred, as *not him*. I saw him as the same as me—we had identical minds. He had the mind of Christ, the same as me. The compassion I now was able to feel for him gave me for the first time in his presence a sense of gentle kindness towards him. I was now joined to him; separation was ended.

He instantly perceived the change in me, and saw too that his attempt to bully me by threat of murder was now powerless. Shortly afterward he left the session.

He called to cancel further sessions. It seemed clear to me he was not yet ready to give up his defenses. His fear of love impelled him to flee. Soon after, his wife also left therapy with me; her fear of her husband was too great. I have every confidence that this man will eventually choose to accept healing. He seems to need more pain before he makes that choice. And I'm confident that his wife, once she gains the inner strength, will give up her need to submit to threat as well.

As I reflect on this matter, I am grateful for the entire experience. I have benefited greatly from it, since now I have absolutely no fear of death. I have shifted my identification from the body to Spirit, and this gives me a great sense of peace.

By the way, it's worth remarking that when this couple initially came to me for therapy, my first impulse was not to take them as patients. In fact, I wouldn't have taken them had I not prayed about it, and received clear guidance from the Holy Spirit that, yes, I was indeed to work with these people. I didn't yet understand why; yet I had come to trust that Love sees what I cannot, working always and unfailingly for the benefit of all. I know now that my work with them was not principally about my patients' healing. It was about my own. And I am so grateful to this man and his wife for being my teachers, my *therapists*, as it were. Because of them, I was able to heal my fear of death. What a wonderful gift they gave me!

* * *

Because you have accepted forgiveness for yourself you now perceive a forgiven world in all its shining beauty. Essentially the beauty results from your having given up your guilt, fear and sense of sin; and therefore you have no need to project any illusory dark thoughts "out there" upon an evil world that you have made up. (T-28.7:2) You then see yourself and all your brothers as innocent, sinless and perfect sons of God. As the loving, final lines of the Forgotten Song (quoted in full above) put it:

> "The light in one awakens it in all. And when you see it in your brother, you *are* remembering for everyone." (T-21.I.10:6-7)

And as the illusionary perception of the world has vanished, and the sense of victimhood vanishes with it, you can then joyfully say:

> "I **am** responsible for what I see.

*I choose the feelings I experience, and I decide upon the goal I would achieve.*
*And everything that seems to happen to me I ask for, and receive as have asked."* (T-21.II.2:3-5)

There being no further need for forgiveness, it too vanishes. (T-27.III.7:1-2) The world becomes a place of hope (T-30.V.2:7), and the yearning for idols ends. (T-30.V.3:2) Also one has given up all hatred and fear as well as the insane idea of sacrifice, or victimhood. (T-21.II.2:3) In essence we have then given up the world. As Jesus says, "You never wanted it." (T-30.9:1-6)

The perception of the Real World that results is thus a symbol of the opposite view of the world we made up (W-8.1,4). There is an awakening from the dream of separation, sin, guilt and fear.

At the Last Chapter of our "Book of Life," the advanced Teacher of God "overlooks the mind and body, seeing only the Face of Christ shining in front of him, correcting all mistakes and healing all perception." (M-22.4:5)

There is a sense of wholeness and the joyful awareness that a forgiven mind results in a healing, holy presence. As *The Song of Prayer* describes it:

"How holy are the healed! For in their sight their brothers share their healing and their love. Bringers of peace,—the Holy Spirit's voice, through whom He speaks for God, Whose Voice He is,—such are God's healers. They but speak for Him and never for themselves. They have no gifts but those they have from God. And those they share because they know that this is what He wills. They are not special. They are holy. They have chosen holiness, and given up all separate dreams of special attributes through which they can bestow unequal gifts on those less fortunate. Their healing has restored their wholeness so they can forgive, and join the song of prayer in which the healed sing of their union and their thanks to God." (S-3.IV.1)

Also, at some point in the Last Chapter,
"Forgiveness vanishes and symbols fade, and nothing that the eyes have seen or ears have heard remains to be perceived. A power wholly limitless has come, not to destroy, but to receive its own." (T-27.III.7:1-2)

The Son of God has given "welcome to the power beyond forgiveness and beyond the world of symbols and of limitations." (T-27.III.7:8) At this point he is aware that every problem is quietly resolved. (T-27.IV.1)
"And the light of Christ in you is given charge of everything you do. For you have brought your weakness unto Him and He has given you His strength instead." (T-31.VIII.2:6-7)

I should like to close this description of what love is by adding two quotes. The first is from the Clarification of Terms:
"How lovely does the world become in just that single instant when you see the truth about yourself reflected there. Now you are sinless and behold your sinlessness. Now you are holy and perceive it so. And now the mind returns to its Creator; the joining of the Father and the

Son, the Unity of unities that stands behind all joining but beyond them all. God is not seen but only understood. His Son is not attacked but recognized."

Finally, here are the affirming words of Jesus:
"Hear me, my brothers, hear and join with me. God has ordained I cannot call in vain, and in His certainty I rest content. For you *will* hear, and you *will* choose again. And in this choice is everyone made free.
I thank You, Father, for these holy ones who are my brothers as they are Your Sons. My faith in them is Yours. I am as sure that they will come to me as You are sure of what they are, and will forever be. They will accept the gift I offer them, because You gave it me on their behalf. And as I would but do Your holy Will, so will they choose. And I give thanks for them. Salvation's song will echo through the world with every choice they make. For we are one in purpose, and the end of hell is near." (T-31. VIII.9:4-7;10)

What a lovely and wonderful prediction for all of us! May we all accept this gift with gratitude.
Peace.

# Appendix
# Martha's Miracle

"Let Him take charge of how you would forgive, and each
occasion then will be to you another step to Heaven and
to peace." (S-III.3:4)

T he above quote from the *Song of Prayer*, scripted by Helen
Schucman in 1977, aptly describes what my wife Martha
decided to do when she found herself unable to love a long-
term friend of ours who lay on the brink of death (and who died
shortly thereafter). I term the process she undertook a "miracle" since the definition of that word in the Course is, "when an
ancient hatred becomes a present love."

The following beautifully written letter was never mailed. It
does, however, graphically and movingly describe the process of
her thought as she gained the willingness to offer up her hatred
to The Holy Spirit, meaningfully desiring the freedom, love and
peace of God. In doing so, she gained "another step to Heaven
and to peace." Thus Martha can be our mentor as we make the
same decision for ourselves.

## The Letter

Dear Norman,

Barbara called with the news. Acute leukemia. Searing words storm my brain. Death. Danger. Loss. Why leukemia? We're age-mates. I could die that way too.

But there is hope. Maybe the doctors' new methods can snatch you from the jaws of death, as they say. I want to help—to send you the power of love and care and strength. I try. I try to see a healing light surrounding you, washing through your veins, cleansing your blood of death. But the images do not come. Instead, old memories come sneaking in, naysayers who cloud my vision, who distract me, who draw me to them with 'buts' that block the path to love.

First comes the memory of learning you had found a way not to pay taxes. I knew you'd made a lot of money, done very well, so why shouldn't you pay taxes? Why shouldn't you pay for the roads you drive on, for the social security you'll collect some day, for the national parks, for the schooling of our country's children, for the agencies that study and rule on the public health—your health? Why shouldn't your dollars go to house the homeless, feed the poor? I felt angry first. Then sad. Disappointed and distant from you. How could you—my friend—do that? It put us miles apart. I thought about it often in the days and weeks after that. I thought maybe I should talk to you, let you know how this affects me. But since we saw each other so seldom I let it pass.

But now it is back, getting in the way of loving you now when you need love. When I need to love you. It stands there blocking my way to you.

Then another shadow from the past appears. So faint at first because it comes from so far back in time. But there it stands shouting, "Look at me!" So long ago. I'll bet you don't remember. We were all so young. A party at George's house. Lots of people I didn't know. The kind of party I really don't like. So much drinking. I was in the kitchen, trying to be helpful I guess. You came in and said something "loving," but with a sexual innuendo that I didn't like. I don't know what else you did—probably nothing much—but you wanted what I didn't want to give. Not anytime, but especially not then, not there.

Barbara was around and I felt what was going on in that space between us must be painful for her. I felt your advances put a distance between her and me and I didn't want that. She was my friend. You were supposed to be my friend too. So why were you putting me in this position? I rebuffed you. Firmly. Then you said to me I should get some therapy to deal with my sexual issues. I don't know what I said or did. Probably told you I was already in therapy. Something defensive. But I was mad. Furious. Who were you to tell me to get therapy because I didn't want what you were trying to get me to do. My God! We were both married. The four of us were friends, right? What way is that to be friends? Yeah, I know this kind of thing happens, but the people involved don't stay friends.

Now here I am forty something years later remembering this ridiculous incident like it was last week. All the angry feelings flooding back at you all over again. Some way to feel about an old friend who has been very near death and isn't out of the woods yet.

I don't want to feel this way. God knows I don't! But how do I get rid of this old baggage that stands in the way? I don't know how. I need help. God knows I need help.

Yes, that's right. God knows. And so I ask God to help me let go of the resentment, the anger, the fear, the disappointment.

I think maybe I know how this works. I can't really ask God to help until I know I really want to let go.

But I really do now. So I sit quietly. Letting out a few deep sighs. Then tears well up and at last I can feel for you again. My thoughts move to embrace you with the love that has made us all friends through the years. I can love you again.

Then gratitude washes over me. Gratitude that I have been released from the burden of resentment that has obscured you from my vision all along.

I'm not sure I'm really all over this yet. But I'll find out if there are tatters of resentment left. They won't be so hard to work on now these big pieces are gone, released to drift backward through time and stay there. Not forgotten, but without the charged emotions that had always enveloped them.

I feel more sure I've left them behind when, a few days later, I chance to think again of us having our little tiff in the kitchen and begin to laugh. It seems now like a scene from a pretty bad novel or a grade B movie. Then I realize that what angered me so was that I believed you were judging me, telling me I had problems, because I didn't want to do what you wanted me to. But I was doing the same thing! Judging you, believing you had problems because you weren't behaving the way I wanted you to. Good old projection. The one we attack is always ourselves.

As for the issue about taxes—well, it seems to have faded away by itself while I wasn't looking. But it has brought me an awareness that there is some larceny in my soul that I keep well hidden. Growing up, I got a strong, clear message that one does what's right (which I guess means moral, fair, humane, lawful) because it's right, whatever the extenuating circumstances. I am grateful to my parents for that lesson, learned from their behavior more than their words. But incorporating that belief into my image of myself has often meant denying the wrongs I do to others in thought or deed because they do not fit the ideal self I want to believe I am.

But in the miraculous way that forgiveness works, having somehow shed the judgment I had made of you I can stop judging myself as well. What freedom there is in giving up assessing the world in terms of good and bad, worthy and unworthy, right and wrong!

Forgiving isn't for those we believe have wronged us. It's always for ourselves, isn't it? In that moment when we let go past hurt, fear, anger, guilt and shame it becomes possible, as the Quakers put it, to "walk cheerfully over the world, answering that of God in everyone."

The distance that kept me from you is gone, Norman. Though you are miles away I feel more connected with you than ever before in our long friendship. I am grateful for that. I am grateful for you.

With love,
Martha
P.S.

Now that Frank and I have been to visit you in the hospital there's more to say.

It was strange—and frustrating—to have to wear protective masks and stay on the far side of your room so you couldn't pick up any germs from us. I wanted to give you a hug, gently, and maybe hold your hand a few minutes as we talked. Not being able to accentuated your fragility, your vulnerability.

Then you spoke of recognizing you had some part to play in what had happened to your body. I think my heart skipped a beat at the poignancy, the sorrow, the wisdom—and the pathos—of that insight.

And so now is a time of learning. A time of profound learning for you as you chart your course in a new direction and see the world and yourself with new vision.

And learning for me as well. That our true calling is to forgiveness. That as we forgive we are forgiven. And therein lies the peace of God.

Well, Norman, as we agreed that day in the hospital, life's gifts sometimes come decked out in some pretty strange wrappings!

Made in the USA
Charleston, SC
13 November 2013